Speech Lessons

Speech Lessons

JOHN MONTAGUE

~

Wake Forest University Press

First American edition published 2012

Wake Forest University Press
Post Office Box 7333
Winston-Salem, NC 27109

Printed on acid-free, recycled paper
in the United States of America

Library of Congress Number 2012930963

ISBN 978-1-930630-59-8 (paperback)

Published in Ireland
by The Gallery Press,
Peter Fallon, Editor

Designed and set in Verdigris
by Nathan W. Moehlmann,
Goosepen Studio & Press

Wake Forest University Press
WWW.WFU.EDU/WFUPRESS

for Rosemary & Paul Kavanagh,
FRIENDLY HOSTS

Contents

PART ONE

One Bright Sunday

One bright Sunday
a duo called for me,
Maurice O'Connell, descendant of . . .
and family historian,
with 'The Pope' O'Mahony,
myriad-stranded genealogist.

They called for me
at my large dank flat
in Northside's Seville Place:
with the white horse
in the fanlight, and
the streetwalkers next door;

last remnants of the old brothel quarter,
Bella Cohen's lurid Nighttown,
plus my own street, Tyrone,
now hushed to silence by the steam
of Amiens' late-night trains
and woken by their dawn whistle;

called to carry me away
to Kildare, Celbridge and Clongowes,
spying on the ghost of the young Joyce –
Are those his initials carved on that desk?
Then splashing in the waxing Liffey:
surely meant as a baptism

for this rustic Northerner
into matters Southern. But
was The Pope's mind gone
or was he great-bearded Pan
capering in the waters
of the Liffey, portly and playful?

Serious but humorous, the young historian
of and from a family laced with eccentrics,
smiled indulgently at the papal antics.
Purling around like a chit
of a child, O my shining stars and body,
down by the dykes of killing Kildare.

None of us really drank,
so we ate chocolate and oranges,
a boyish feast, on the river bank
before plunging into the *hitherandthithering*
waters of, again. Bless my messengers both
who redeemed that long-ago Sunday

gifting me with a new kind of innocence:
that grown-ups of some importance
may still frolic like infants.

Speech Lesson

for Michael Longley

1

The chant of those carriage wheels
as we chug towards Belfast;
clickety-click, lickety-split,
When will I learn again to speak?

A straggle of villages before Dungannon:
Beragh, Carrickmore, Sixmilecross
(forlorn stations, later bypassed)
or *Will I never, ever speak again?*

2

THE FLOWER

After hilly Dungannon, holy Donaghmore.
A cluster of convent girls clambers
aboard the train, sweep and swirl
past the place of the tongue-tied boy
who huddles his head in his book
(which suddenly sheds all importance)
while they pile into the next compartment.
A chatter-and-clatter like starlings
as they settle. But one, bolder,
tiptoes along the swaying corridor
to risk a look where he sits, blushing.
Then another. A flurry of giggles.
Though as the troop leaves, prodding one another,
the bold one turns to throw him a flower.

3

Under the leather seats the creak
of iron wheels as we steam towards Belfast:
When will I learn again to speak?
The Calvin Mills at Portadown,
Balmoral Showgrounds, and tethered
above the wartime city, a silvery barrage balloon.
(Belfast's knell had not yet rung.)

4

Near the bulky City Hall, 20 Wellington.
An ardent young Englishwoman,
speaking of War and Poetry,
places a hand on his tummy-tum-tum,
(the first stranger to have so done).
'Young man, learn to speak from your diaphragm:
Many merry men marched many times.
And you should read Drummond Allison.
He was stationed here in Northern Ireland.'
She presses down, again and again:
'Consider our King: he broadcasts, stammering.
So let the wind whistle through your lungs.
And read poetry aloud, it can be such fun!
From how far away did you say you've come?'

5

Clickety-click, clickety-clack as
the Derry evening train ferries him back
all the way to County Tyrone and
Beragh station, a lantern swaying
along the platform. The parting whistle.
Then the long pull on his bicycle
through the hay-scented countryside
to the turf-heavy hearth at home,
the Rosary and a mug of Ovaltine
in the Sacred Heart-flushed kitchen.
Candle in hand, he climbs to his room.
A scurry of giggles, the shock of that flower.
Many weary men marched many times:
Shall I begin to speak again?

I can still smell her perfume.

Adam's Apple

after Cranach

Her skin is smooth
as peach or appleblossom –
or a snakeskin.

The snake's fangs gleam,
the fruit glistens
as warmly in her palm

as ever it shone
on the holy tree.
He savours it

so slowly
it sticks in
our throat forever.

A Memory of Nuala

Once, idling in Stephen's Green,
with wandering steps and slow,
we fell to kissing, but
were ordered to leave,

our cheeks burning,
by a baleful guardian:
not cherubim with
flashing swords,

nor a radiant archangel
with wide warm wings,
but a runty Dublin official.
Expelled again from Eden:

rapt, *in soft sexual delusion*,
no wonder we love Blake's 'Milton'!

The Wild Irish Goat

I have met a bearded billy in the heather,
horns curving back like scimitars,
and once high on the flank of Mweelrea
I came face-to-face, to our surprise,
with one of Ireland's rarest ladies.

Through the amber embrasure of her eyes
the she-goat surveyed me, then leaped
away down the rocky mountainside,
snorting. To warn her flock to move on:
she had seen and smelt a human.

Scarecrow

for John Shinnors

Scarecrows grow scarce
since we no longer till fields.

Funereal figures
standing in the midst of harvest,

they flapped wildly in the wind
though never moved.

They wore the old clothes
of the dead men of the household

with sometimes a cap or a hat
which would often blow off.

Crossed staves in a field,
a home-made crucifixion,

or the gaunt autumnal brother
of the rotund snowman.

~

But I forgot the shrewdness
of the carrion crow. Before
the crop was gathered in
I swear I saw more than one
of those jagged black birds
happily settle on the arm
of that structure meant to warn.

Baldung's Vision

I saw a tiny Christ
caper on the cross

silent as a salamander
writhing in fire

or a soldier triumphant
when the battle's lost;

wine bursts from
his body's grapeskin:

'The suffering you see
is our daily mystery,

so follow my body
as it sings mutely

(a lantern, a ladder,
a window, a pathway)

of pain calcined away
in a dance of ecstasy.'

A Resigned President

On a summer evening, beyond Sneem,
   we discuss your resignation,
the memoir you hope to write. Again
   I observe your gentleness,
that absence of meanness, or of malice
   which left you helpless

before the silent bite of the terrier
   with his small teeth,
the arid legality of the Law Professor,
   putting you in your place,
who held our highest, where honour shines,
   a credit to our race.

We joked lightly about your bardic name,
   a disgrace to the Ó Dálaighs,
you laughed, *not even a poor poet*,
   and I felt the shame
of your being slighted by a Maenad
   citing Dante's Celestine.

Maundy Thursday. As in the old dispensation
   we saw the floodgates open,
that same valley cowled in mourning,
   as your resigned body
was laid down, the spirit leaping towards
   the light you believed in.

All night blue flames flickered in
   the de Vere stained glass
above the high altar, the oak coffin,
   and in the chill morning
hosts assemble across Ireland to attend him,
   like a murdered king.

With Chopin's funeral march resounding in
the hushed streets of Sneem,
that watchful ring of snowy mountains,
a solemn salute of guns
as a still young nation comes to attention
to honour him.

But military pomp and precision dwindle
in the wind's fierce requiem.
As Hillery speaks, the fury of the rain
hardens to hail:
our land's grief is manifest; they offended us,
offending him.

Cearbhall, *duine uasal*, open-minded Christian,
generous, unjudging spirit,
your merry smile made all the clichés true:
blossom of the sweet branch,
delightful, for a summer while, to have broken
bread with you

who spoke over Ó Ríordáin, who spoke over Ó Riada
in St Gobnait's of Ballyvourney,
and now you have joined that ghostly procession
always moving on
from our still unresolved republic of pain,
rehearsing the problem.

Leap

i.m. John Berryman

John, I refuse to dilate upon
your *saltus dei*, your leap to death,
but merely attest to a coincidence:
I read of it on the Aer Lingus plane
that ferried me away from my first wife.
I retreated to a corner seat and cried
while a telegram arrived at my forsaken
Paris flat, from chill Minneapolis,
codenamed: *Death by Ice*.

A Long Line

A valediction for Verling

Plaiting one long leg over the other
John Verling sits, a drinking man,
settled in some warm snug-corner
with his sloe black pint before him.

But also a draughtsman,
perched high in Cork's City Hall,
though longing, above all,
to withdraw to West Cork

where your spiderly line
traced the nettled doorways
of mouldering whitewashed cottages:
a connoisseur of deserted villages,

and sagging rafters, but
also of opulent breasts
and buttocks, the up-and-at-it
of Merriman's 'Midnight Court'

or my own Florentine frolics.
Dolci amici, addio!
I recall our early days
in the Wild West of Ballydehob

chugging out to some deserted isle,
lugging pints of rough wine,
then swimming stark naked,
your children and mine.

Blessed in our brief glimpse
of a West Cork Eden,

may I be allowed to imagine
some snug-corner of heaven

where Gabriel pulls a slow
pint, and John unfurls his long legs,
downs a draught, and bends
to draw a long, slow line.

Leisure Centre

Moving from the cool to the hot pool
I follow a star, flashing across the sky;
no, not a star, but an incoming plane
with, yes, there beyond it, the evening star!
If I stayed here longer I would no longer
know what abiding things are . . .

Silences

for Elizabeth

1

Poetry is a weapon, and should be used,
though not in the crudity of violence.
It is a prayer before an unknown altar,
a spell to bless the silence.

2

There is a music beyond all this,
beyond all forms of grievance,
where anger lays its muzzle down
into the lap of silence.

3

Or some butterfly script,
fathomed only by the other,
as supple fingers draw
a silent message from the tangible.

Vendange

for Pierre Joannon

Mists and mellow fruitfulness —
as we cycle through the dawn
along the great river Marne,
a pal from still-dormant Derry
and myself, passing out each other,
sturdy Raleigh against low-slung Racer,

to toil all day among the vines
shearing the grapes with the claws,
the jaws of the iron secateurs,
then hoisting our cloudy burden
of green-gold champagne grapes
in their great woven baskets.

Close bosom-friend of the maturing sun —
the harvest heat beat down
bold and brazen as a gong,
but we were wild and young,
Keats and Rimbaud in my rucksack,
On n'est pas sérieux, quand on a dix-sept ans.

~

Our reward, to dance and sing in
the village square each evening
to the yearning cadence of an accordion,
our arms that all day curved round
rush baskets curve now round waists.
Though as midnight strikes the girls
melt away, laughing faintly, and
we ride back to our spartan hostel.

Sundays we tramped the countryside,
two lanky Irish lads, slowly growing aware
of what desolation had been wrought there,
the earth trenched with wounds:
for beyond the local *Monuments aux Morts*
sprawled Allied and German cemeteries
stored with vintage blood, strange wineries.
La terre est nubile et débordé de sang.

While barred clouds bloom the soft-dying day —
the punctual magic of the train,
each evening the long, lit Rheims Express
passing through on her way to Paris,
listening to the carriages' swaying clatter
I did not yet know they were ferrying
my own future towards and away from me.
Le Soleil, le foyer de tendresse et de vie.

Keats and Rimbaud jostling in my rucksack,
On est trop sérieux, quand on a dix-huit ans!

A Hit at Hardy

Old Thomas Hardy,
I be ashamed of thee;
writing of true love only
when she slept 'neath the tree.

Your costive love hobbled
decades of English lyric;
gave our shared Muse
a dose of physic.

Larkin learnt from you
how not to love
and when it was over
to hardly forgive:

between proud Yeats
and your so humble craft
there is an arrogance –
– yours, alas!

In your parched
lyric only dead love exists,
but in Willy Yeats
there is sweet permanence.

When in your remorseful
verses love was rerun,
you spoke, alive, alone
above her skeleton.

Through the rotting coffin
boards she could not hear
the words she longed for,
in her young and pulsing years.

Grandfather God

Hugo saw God playing with us, his grandchildren;
a good grey grandfather, listening and marvelling,
to laugh without frightening, play without harming,
Riez sans faire peur, jouez sans faire mal:
the old poet exhorts the boisterous children.

But a Papal bull bellows *Ineffabilis!*
Everything is sullied: to deny so, Godless:
Tout est souillure, et qui le nie est un athée.
Where man cries 'Love' Heaven replies 'Sin';
evil infects the cradle of the newly born.

Péché! Péché! Le mal est dans les nouveau-nés!
All the cradles are black, save the starlit one;
all women bear shame, with one exception:
so the power-encrusted Church has spoken,
exalting the Virgin as their rival Queen.

I will not accept this exception.
The womb is blameless as the strangeness
she bears. And every 'burning babe'
falls through a broken hymen.
The divine and the human are interwoven:

Behold Jesus, a carpenter's son.

PART TWO

In My Grandfather's Mansion

John Montague JP (1840–1907) and family

'Merciful God! In what a frightful condition was the country at that time. I speak now of the North of Ireland. It was there, indeed, the seat of Orange ascendancy and irresponsible power. To find a justice of the peace not an Orangeman would have been an impossibility.'

— William Carleton, *Autobiography* (1869)

'The poor Irishman lives in the simple house of his childhood
with the well-known neighbors and faces,
They warmly welcome him, he is barefoot again . . .'

— Walt Whitman, 'The Sleepers', *Leaves of Grass* (1855)

Prologue

PROPRIETOR

From a corner, from above the paraffin tins,
I hoisted a black-and-white sign
of mouldering wood:
JOHN MONTAGUE, PROP.

Now, small head of the household,
I hauled out the shutters each evening
to board up the Shop and Post Office,
with panels larger than myself.

Singing in the summer twilight
when the job was done,
singing to my weary aunts,
singing to the wild Lynches

across the way, singing
to the Clarkes, 'on the next block',
singing to the cows in their stalls,
singing to the pigs in their *cró*,

singing to the hens
settling onto their roosts,
singing to old Tim
clopping in his stable:

October winds lament
Around the castle of Dromore,
But peace is in her lofty halls,
My dearest treasure stor'd . . .

A solitary minstrel
of family dreams, with

my private menagerie
of ghosts and animals,

my unbroken boy soprano
breaking the membrane of the gloaming,
that sign of ownership
at my feet: JOHN MONTAGUE, PROP.

Dread spirits of the Blackwater,
Clann Owen's wild banshee . . .

~

My grandfather comes riding by.
I see his glorious long beard
as he sits in his sidecar or
jaunts in his pony and trap.

He hails me, 'But John!
That was always *my* name:
look at that wooden sign.
Yet you may carry it on,

and please keep singing.
I heard you summon
Clann Owen's wild banshee:
she has always followed our family.

Take time to thrive, my ray of hope,
in the gardens of Dromore,
take heed, young eaglet, till your wings
are feathered fit to soar . . .'
He cracks his reins, and disappears.

~

A bare-legged boy,
I crouch on my *creepie* stool,
on the edge of the reddening hearth
and stare up the open chimney
to where, through turf smoke, I spy
clouds like galleons coursing by.
Or scramble up the stairs to where
a windowless room shelters
the remnants of his library.
The candle flame trembles as I read,
rocking in his cushioned chair
as if John Montague, JP, were still there,
pondering his many volumes, instead of me,
a Brooklyn urchin, troubling his lair.

In My Grandfather's Mansion

I

In my grandfather's library
there were many volumes,

Bibles massive as flagstones,
heavy print my eye could trawl along:

the thunder of the *Old Testament*.

I climbed the Mount with Moses,
stood in the presence of the Lord,
or listened as he spake from a cloud.

For, lo, I had suffered the long exodus
from Brooklyn and New York
where they worshipped the Golden Calf

which now staggers, newly born,
rasped clean by its mother's tongue,
on the cobblestones of our farmyard.

2

I chanted the *Proverbs and Psalms*
and later bathed in the *Song of Songs*:

Thy love is headier than wine,
honey and milk lie under thy tongue,
thy lips . . . drip as the honeycomb.

To what dark-eyed maiden
might I yet sing such a song?

Lily of the valley, rose of Sharon . . .

3

Matthew, Mark, Luke and John
blessed the bed I lay upon.

My grandfather's bed in my grandfather's room;
but I loved the *Revelations* of yet another John,

he of Patmos: *a woman clothed with the sun,*
a two-horned lamb who spoke like a dragon —

Locusts, with breastplates of iron;
the heads of the horses as heads of lions.

The *Apocalypse*, God's Horror Comic!
Like the scary film, with Boris Karloff,

I had seen on my last day in Brooklyn
and can remember as the rats scamper

above the damp-blotched wallpaper
in the shadowy rafters over my head.

The beams of our house are cedar,
and our rafters of fir . . .

John Whale's *House of the Dead*
seen by a small boy, now transplanted.

4

Christmas stars stud the sky
as in my grandfather's bed I lie.

'What are you doing in my bedroom,
plundering my library, perusing my will?
Where the devil did you come from?'

'John begat James who begat John.
Why did you sire so many children,
you old goat, with luxuriant beard
and sideburns? I am second generation
fruit of your loins, who has come from afar
to dwell with your two maiden daughters,
your eldest, Brigid, your youngest, Winifred,
in that rural empire you founded.'

'Like Ruth amid the alien corn!'

'Except I was born in Depression Brooklyn,
a raw raucous place you have never seen,
with clanging trolleys and lurid neon.'

'So you were born in America
where they had that terrible Civil War:
Meagher of the Sword, at Fredericksburg,
where over a thousand Irish died,
sporting "their sprigs of green".

'Look at those photographs of slaughtered
soldiers, arranged by Mathew Brady,
next to Whitman, in my library.'

'With Butler's *Lives of the Saints*
and Vasari's *Lives of the Artists*:
at least you were catholic in your tastes!'

'And in my thoughts: Cardinals Wiseman
and Manning, conducting their lofty debates
around the Immaculate Conception,
ponderous and Victorian to you, perhaps.
Though Catholic, I served the Queen
as postmaster and lay magistrate:
a bleak land, after the Famine.
No need to read the Riot Act
(white gloves often on the bench),
a small cog in the Imperial machine:
the greatest Empire ever seen.'

'And, lo, led your people out of Egypt,
downhill, that is, from Altamuskin,
and Altcloghfin, to this Broad Road
that sweeps from Derry to Belfast.'
(Years later, in troubled dreams,
I hear ghostly carriages rumble past.)

5

'My grandfather's clock was too tall for the shelf
so he spent forty years in the bed,
going tick-tock, tick-tock,
until he stopped short,
never to go again
in Garvaghey graveyard.'

Many years without slumbering
(Tick-tock, tick-tock),
many children engendering . . .
I saw his grave dug open
to admit another daughter,
sired in that same iron bed
I now occupy, listening
to the rodents rustling overhead.

His thigh bone seemed enormous,
large as the *jawbone of an ass*,
but I was only an altar boy
clothed in mystic surplice and soutane
(over New World knickerbockers)
to serve her Funeral Mass, before
the fresh clods struck the coffin,
brass handles, polished wood.
For dust thou art,
and unto dust shalt thou return . . .

6

'That ditty should have stuck in your throat!
Why must you strike such a vulgar note?
Without me you would not even exist,
so a little courtesy would not go amiss!'

'Listen, you auld fecker, you may be my grandfather
but the round world has rolled on since then.'

'And completely lost its manners?'

'You had Cardinals: Manning, Wiseman, Newman,
ruminating over the Immaculate Contraption.
My heroes were Tiger Flowers, and Slapsy
        Maxy Rosenbloom,
and then the Brown Bomber, and Billy Conn;
livelier than your solemn, red-hatted procession.
Did you never play stoop-ball, put nickels under
        trolley or tram?'

'Brash as an American, you don't sound
like my grandson, or even an Ulsterman!
Do you know Newman's definition of a Gentleman?
"A Gentleman is one who never inflicts pain" —
Study that for a while, then speak to me again.
Besides, large families were common then.'

'But what would your poor wife have to say?'

7

But who was my grandmother?
Silence. Or almost.
Her name I learnt was Quinn
(pronounced, locally, *Queen*),
the robust one of several sisters
afflicted with consumption,
wasting away slowly, slowly
in the house across from our own.

(The Lynches and I played
in its ruins, wrestling in our dungarees
amidst swollen grainsacks as
bats looped through broken windows;
unaware of where we were, walls
blighted by illness, now
shrunken to a storehouse
for horses, cattle, hay.)

And I have only one photograph
of a tightly corseted woman.
She unlaced them ritually
for my grandfather's embrace
in this same iron bed,
night after patriarchal night,
until she died, in childbirth.

A grandparent myself,
I say a word for her now,
a silent, solemn figure
lost in the shadows
of a doomed place:
before she crosses the road,
through the portals of our house,
into male energy and merriment.

In my grandmother's time, one woman
was Queen of the known world
(another, Virgin Queen of the unknown),
so shall I name her our Lost Queen,
Our Lady of Shadows, Our Lady of 'Shall Not',
a patient figure at her spinning wheel
without whom I would not have been?

8

'Out of the darkness I dare to speak.
I am not the silent Queen
of Garvaghey and Altcloghfin,
I am not a plaster saint,
I am not a figurine.

'If my John can speak
across a century's silence,
why should I stay mute:
I was a flesh-and-blood woman,
the strongest of my house,
so do not distil me into dream!

'But how the men were spoilt,
grouped in the parlour,
scarcely bothering to lift their plates
to help us when we served,
dunting like sucking calves
as we ladled out their portions,
then back to the talk and drink again.'

(And, abashed, I recall
a rare flash of anger from Aunt Brigid:
'All the men together, playing cards
and drinking whiskey, while
we hungry children cried.')

9

Whitman saw Ireland 'an ancient sorrowful mother,
once a queen, now lean and tatter'd . . .'
'Will you have a titter of wit, man,

or I'll push you before my besom.
There were mouths agape, bottoms to clean,
cows to milk, and churns to turn,

a hearth-crook heavy with pots and pans,
farls of soda and wheaten bread.
I was far smarter than most men,

though I left all the gabble to them.
And you seem to forget I loved my John,
he was a fine figure of a man,

handsome as Victoria's German one:
Did you know that every night in Windsor
Albert's clothes were laid out on the bed,

and she slept with his picture over her head?
She presided over her unfurling world:
India, Africa, the Crimea and Khartoum,

as I presided over mine, Garvaghey, Altcloghfin,
pressing the treadles of my sewing machine.
So wasn't I happy to have my John

and that lively bunch of children?
And wasn't he the great reader,
though only a class of hedge schoolmaster?

(That scringe of chalk on slate.)
He was so pleased when Cousin Joseph
became a Cardinal, with his book on Prophet John.

And who are you, anyway, you whippersnapper,
sharing our family secrets with the world:
so I say again, have a titter of wit, man!'

PART THREE

Patience and Time

Many Mansions

In my grandfather's house there were many mansions.

In the dim back shelves of the shop
lay serried rows of dicky bows.
Where were the gentlemen who wore them?
Arrayed in Garvaghey graveyard in rows . . .

I hid in one of the empty tea chests
inhaling the aroma of India or China
where a great war was waging as
I crinkled the strips of tin foil.

A squat barrel of molasses
stood in the cellar, exuding a thick sweetness
like the dull nectar of wasps,
while from their dank corner
the sickly white tendrils of
the seed potatoes strained
towards the almost lunar light
of the spider-gauzed window.

But most ghostly, the line of mannequins
along the long shed. Those women
who had once sported antique hats, lace blouses,
long skirts, even ball gowns,
now endured my embrace of their wire limbs,
a small boy sticking his fingers into their metal midriffs
as I ferried them from place to place.

I tried to dance with them
but the metal scraped and tangled
in our slow stiff waltz,
so I toppled them over one by one
until they lay still as the dicky bows on their shelf.

Disappointments

Trudging home along
that broad road
which led to and from
that new school
to which I had been sent
against my will
by my younger aunt,
and having found
Glencull not so bad after all

I gathered flowers
the whole way home,
plucking them from
the thorny crevices
of the ditch:
primrose, daisy,
buttercup, bluebell,
the weak milk thistle;
homely and humble,
they still seemed
a real peace offering.

But when I gave it to her
she did not look
but took, and flung
it abruptly outside
onto the dunghill,
a small disappointment
that still stings.

But now I think
perhaps it was
a bigger disappointment
for her, no longer
a dancing girl
given bouquets
by gallant men
but only wildflowers
by a little boy.

Fodder

Cold evenings, as I carried
bristling bundles of straw
from the haggard or
barn to the byre
where the cattle waited,
jangling their chains,
fretful as children in
their wooden stalls,

her path would
often cross mine:
tracks of boots,
trails of straw,
strewing the ground,
from byre to barn –
runic signs of
silent affection.

Patience and Time

Winifred Montague (1900–1983)

Patience and time
will bring the snail
to Jerusalem . . .
my Aunt Winifred's favourite saying
as she sits playing Patience

after she had spent hours
mucking out the byre,
wearing man's boots or wellies,
then straddling the runnel
to wash it down.

Or wheeling the barrow
heavy with dung to
the mound of the dunghill:
hardly the occupation
for a bright convent girl
summoned all the way
from college quad to farmyard
when Ireland divided
and her brothers slid into bankruptcy.

(Or balanced on a stool,
leaning against the warm
flank of a feeding heifer,
squeezing and squirting
the swollen teats until
they fill the frothing pail.)

Patience and time
bring the snail to Jerusalem:

I see the tiny pilgrim
on his gleaming liquid course;
his periscopic horns,
his silver slide forward.

(Or whirling the churn,
the slosh of the cream,
until a yellow gleam
lights the small window:
I glimpse the Golden Dome
of his tireless dream.)

In the winter evenings,
Patience, or Solitaire,
by the tilley lamp.
Card falls on card
upon the baize table:
no matter how hard
there is no complaint,
no thunder against fate.

As numbers mount
from Ace to Ten,
according to suit,
and a red row climbs
beside the black:
Spades against Diamonds,
Clubs against Hearts,
Queens fall on Jacks,
Kings fall on Queens

and the snail halts.

Home Coming

Another routine chore,
rounding up the strays:
a heifer near calving
sheltered by the lime kiln;
another gadabout which has clambered
high along a heathery slope,

while the older cows huddle
around the starting gate,
waiting to be escorted home
between hawthorn hedges.
They nuzzle and nibble
fresh leaves, long roadside grass,

ignoring the switch across
their broad passive backs:
their sly revenge, a gush
and swish of warm manure,
splattering happily as infants
as they enter the home stretch,

the closing gates of byre, farm.
Then a rattle of chains as
they resume their positions,
crunching fodder from the rack,
attending the further relief
of a deft milker's fingers,

as my bone-tired aunt

bends to her evening task.
Soon the cattle will
bed down in their stalls.
A storm lamp dangles
from the rafters as
twilight closes in.

Is that a child asleep
in the crib of straw,
or a trick of the light?

Devotions

for Father Ken Letts

After October Devotions
cigarette-tips glowed
as my old neighbours
jostled at the chapel gates
or under the big tree,
for their shy autumnal chat
before their bicycle lamps
drew wobbly circles
upon the darkness while
they flowed homewards
over the country roads,
to Brackagh, Tychany,
Rarogan and Altcloghfin.

(From the gaslit church
the sound of Aunt Winifred
running once again through
an old hymn, 'Faith of Our Fathers'
or '*Tantum Ergo Sacramentum*',
on the creaking harmonium.)

Folding my surplice,
sometimes I joined them,
sometimes raced home.
If I were to return now
would their friendly shades
part to receive me,
offering a light from
a frail match shielded
in an old jacket's fold?

Hillside

'They'll never have this house',
my taciturn Aunt Winifred cries,
straightening her back on the hillside
where we were comradely spreading turf.
An old-fashioned, heart-piercing cry,
all the way from the Sagas.
But somehow ringing true
to this little Brooklyn boy
as we halt to gaze down
across fields of alien corn,
to my new, mysterious home.

The Long Hangar

for the O'Mearas

1

The long hangar of the turf shed
faces the Broad Road where cars whine.
There our winter warmth is stored,

as all summer long the small carts
come lumbering down from
what we still call 'The Mountain':

high-packed cribs, painted sides and wheels,
a jangle of harness along narrow lanes,
as winkered Tim plods stolidly home.

2

There were three kinds of turf:

rough heads, sliced only one sod deep,
with a tuft of heather on the top,
sentinels at the rear of the hearth;

the *fúms* were long, light and dry.
They were first to start the fire,
kindling with immediate heat and light;

the boghole turf, deep and tobacco-dark,
burning as slowly as coal. Ash-smoored,
they smouldered, a ruddy glow, till morning.

3

When my cousins came in the summer
we played under the echoing roof.
Kings of the Castle, perched high

atop our terraced, musty realm,
we inhaled that almost cathedral smell,
while pelting each other with dusty sods of turf.

4

Ere long, the girdered hangar of the turf shed's
corrugated iron would be hauled down, its ghost

engulfed by the ever-widening Broad Road:
not horse, or pony-and-cart, but long distance lorries,

indifferent to dogs and infants, as they
barrel from Londonderry, through Omagh, to Belfast;

the future, already whirling past.

Acknowledgements and Notes

Acknowledgements are due to the editors of the following magazines, periodicals, and books where some of these poems, or versions of them, were published first: *Agenda*, *Best of Irish Poetry 2008* (Southword Editions), *Earth Voices Whispering: An Anthology of Irish War Poetry 1914–1945* (edited by Gerald Dawe, Blackstaff, 2008), *Franco-Irish Connections* (Four Courts Press, 2009), *The Irish Times*, *Journal of the Bray Cualann Historical Society* (Cearbhall Ó Dálaigh Centenary Issue), *Love Poet, Carpenter: Michael Longley at Seventy* (Enitharmon, 2009), *Many Mansions* (Ireland Chair of Poetry Trust and Stoney Road Press, 2009), *The New Yorker*, *Poetry Ireland Review*, and *The Times Literary Supplement*.

In My Grandfather's Mansion was published in 2009 in a limited edition by The Gallery Press.

PAGE 13

Eoin ('The Pope') O'Mahony (1904–1970), Knight of Malta, a barrister with a screw loose, was a much beloved eccentric in the Dublin of my youth, garrulous and white-bearded. When Brendan Behan was in gaol in England, for example, Eoin sent a telegram declaring, 'The Pope is Coming!' 'Meet the Clans', a radio programme on which he was resident genealogist, attended to various Irish families, including his own.

PAGE 22

Hans Baldung (c.1484–1545) was a mystical Renaissance German artist who sometimes saw 'God's death as but a play', a doctrine probably found in the Apocryphal Gospels.

PAGE 23

Cearbhall Ó Dálaigh (1911–1978) resigned as President of Ireland in 1976, after being called 'a thundering disgrace' by the Minister for Defence because he had opposed an Emergency Powers Bill introduced by Taoiseach Liam Cosgrave, fearing it would undermine civil liberties. In the *Inferno*, III, 59–60, Celestine resigns as Pope, making what Dante calls 'the great refusal', a phrase used disparagingly of Ó Dálaigh by Máire Mhac an tSaoi, a prominent poet in Irish, and daughter of Seán MacEntee, the sharpest tongue in the Fianna Fáil party.